Grandmom's Encounters

Grandmom Gets Visitors!

Joy Zummell

Edited by C. Freeman

Library of Congress Control Number: 2016930474
[Windsail Publishing], [Lincoln]

ISBN: 10:1-943071-01-2

ISBN:13:978-1-943071-01-2

windsailpub@gmail.com

joyzummell@gmail.com

DEDICATION

This book is dedicated to loving parents and
grandparents everywhere.

Acknowledgements

Thanks to all of the grandchildren
who express love for their
grandmother and inspired this book.

Grandmom was so happy!

So Grandmom brings out the doll.

She brings out the toy car.

She brings out the Toy truck.

Then, she brings out her candy.

CHOCOLATE

She brings out the bike.

Why is Grandmom so happy?

Special visitors were here!

When we are ready for more fun, Grandmom brings out the books.

Then, she gets the bubbles.

Grandmom loves to watch us
make mud pies.

When everything is quiet, Grandmom
tells us stories about her house plants.

The plants are presents to Grandmom;
so she   keeps them growing with extra care!

Grandmom let us sleep with her.

It is a fun day!

www.ingramcontent.com/pod-product-compliance
Lightning Source LLC
Chambersburg PA
CBHW041756050426
42443CB00023B/21